LIVING UPROOTED

Companion Workbook

⇒MARI EYGABROAD⇐

www.marieygabroad.com

Dedicated to the Lord,

to my husband, Bryan,

to our children Matthias and Isabella,

and our children in heaven, Hope, Joy, and Adia.

CONTENTS

CHAPTER 1

SUBMITTING TO GOD'S PLAN

THEME: SUBMISSION

A FTER ABOUT SIX YEARS of serving overseas, my husband and I sensed God moving to change our missionary service. But nothing pushed us out of the job my husband was doing or the country we served. We loved what we were doing and the people we were serving. So, we reached out to a mentor, who introduced us to the discernment process—inviting people to pray on our behalf regarding God's direction.

My husband was offered an instructor position we believed would be a perfect fit, and we were excited to take it. We invited ten people to pray for us. When we followed up with them a few weeks later, those who had heard from God confirmed that we should take the position, yet the timing remained a mystery. Wisely, we heeded their counsel not to set a timeline but to let God lead.

Among the many benefits of inviting others into your decision-making are access to the wisdom of others and a more objective approach. We accepted the offer and thought we would be moving within a year. Three years later, we were still waiting. Circumstances beyond our control hindered our path forward. Sometimes, we questioned whether we had heard God correctly, but reflecting on our discernment process gave us confident patience. Confirmation we received for our direction, both personally and from those not vested in the decision, served as an anchor holding our faith fast, as we held our plans loosely and trusted God to work out the timing.

When discerning God's plans for our lives, we are wise to humble ourselves and submit to God and our elders, allowing them to speak into our lives. Trying to determine God's call on our lives without inviting others into the process reflects pride. James 4:6 quotes Proverbs 3:34: "God resists the proud, but gives grace to the humble" (NKJV). That sentiment is repeated in 1 Peter 5:5: "In the same way, you who are younger, submit yourselves to your elders. All of you, clothe yourselves with humility toward one another, because, 'God opposes the proud but shows favor to the humble'" (NIV).

Key Scripture

Come now, you who say, "Today or tomorrow we will go into such and such a town and spend a year there and trade and make a profit"—yet you do not know what tomorrow will bring. What is your life? For you are a mist that appears for a little time and then vanishes. Instead you ought to say, "If the Lord wills, we will live and do this or that."

James 4:13–15

Supporting Scripture

Proverbs 15:22, 16:3

Keywords

Advice, Counsel, Discernment, Hold Loosely, Submission, Patience, Plans, Prayer, Pride

Treasure Hunt

Choose a keyword that describes an area in which you are feeling confident. Write in your journal how you see yourself moving forward and leading others in that area.

Choose another keyword that describes an area in which you want to grow. Begin by writing a prayer to the Lord, seeking wisdom, direction, and steps to help you follow Him in that area. Next, write down one to three action steps you can implement today. Finally, find three verses in Scripture that speak to this area of growth, and write them in your journal.

Action Steps

Submit your plans for the next weeks or months to a few people who will pray to God about the plans and speak honestly with you. Explain to those people that you need to hear what the Lord is saying to others on your behalf. Set a date to follow up with them in a couple of weeks.

Choose a simple way to surrender your plans to the Lord. Consider these possibilities:

- Write them on a rock and throw the rock into a body of water.

- Write them on a piece of paper and burn the paper.

- Paint them on a canvas and paint over them.

Be creative and choose an act of submission that fits your creative style. Once you've surrendered your plans to the Lord, open your hands to receive His plans for you.

Prayer

Father God, I submit my hopes, dreams, and plans to You. I release them to You, and I am keeping my hands open to receive the plans You have for me. Please show me the people You have placed in my life who will help reveal Your plans to me. Give me the courage to ask others to pray about my plans, and give me an open mind to receive what they hear from You. Here I am, Lord. Lead me. I pray in Jesus's name. Amen.

Keyword Search

Just to have a little fun and reinforce those keywords,

here's a little word search for you.

SUBMISSION

ADVICE, COUNSEL, DISCERNMENT, HOLD LOOSELY,

PATIENCE, PLANS, PRAYER, PRIDE, SUBMISSION

```
C G J C O U N S E L Y D W U F B H Q A F
K W O P A T I E N C E V I P M R I Y N L
L X K O W O R B U L N E U J U V B W J I
V Y B T L P R A Y E R M Q H F O R V W V
C P Z W B R U R H X T S D C T Q N N N L
N N Q C F I Z F U O D U V S O Y V A L Q
C M M T L D F C B K I B H O C B K G A V
G Z I J W E B U E Y S M N U J H F B D Z
P P L A N S E H G T C I F O Z Q Z E V K
P X V Y N A P A H G E S Z D V K N G I K
F L V T Y O B V L A R S B H L D Y S C R
I P N J J R S N N O N I C Z F R V J E O
B O X M E O M S F X M O H T I T V H U Z
L Y B D U L W K Q O E N Z Z W T S X X P
Q A J P Y N F C W P N I W C M Y T S P U
O T F B A I N F X I T K M W G D J P A H
J H G V P T J T I P R F Y O I M C I N I
H O L D L O O S E L Y I Q C U L P U K O
I L R P G H R J I X X V K I R Y K O Q C
Y N N V T N H V A R G W K F I W B C O G
```

CHAPTER 2

FINDING IDENTITY IN CHRIST

THEME: IDENTITY

P ART OF A MOTHER's job is to help her children find their identity and forge their paths in life. Unfortunately, just as I entered my menstrual cycle when I was twelve years old, my mother passed away. My father didn't know how to talk to me about sex, tampons, and being a girl. Without guidance, parts of my identity that were beginning to form remained unclear.

I was sixteen before I discovered, through an embarrassing moment with a classmate, that I did not have proper hygiene and should probably use deodorant. I had awkward social skills, and it was challenging to make friends. Thankfully, as I gained life skills, my social awkwardness dissipated. I was making friends, but clarity about my identity seemed beyond reach. I just became who others told me to be.

When I was twenty-six, I married my first husband, who left me for another woman after four years. I thought my world was ending, and I struggled to know who I was if not a wife. God brought a couple into my life who walked me through that heartache and eventually became like parents to me. They helped me discover what it meant to find my identity in Christ.

After a few years of being single again, God orchestrated my relationship with Bryan. We don't seek to find our identity in one another. Our relationship is centered around God, and we are both confident in who we are as His children. Sadly, we lost three children to miscarriage and stillbirth during our time overseas. Once again, the enemy who always lurks nearby tried to make me question my identity. While the losses were devastating, I would have lost my identity entirely if I had allowed childbearing to forge it.

The thought of losing loved ones is uncomfortable. But when I ask myself if I will still love God when inevitable loss happens, the answer is yes. Sure, grief will likely bring anger and confusion. I will have to figure out how to move on. I confidently believe, though, that loss will drive me to press into God all the more.

Key Scripture

See what great love the Father has lavished on us, that we should be called children of God! And that is what we are! The reason the world does not know us is that it did not know him.

1 John 3:1 NIV

Supporting Scripture

Proverbs 3:5–6; John 12:43; 1 Corinthians 12:14–20; Colossians 3:2–3, 3:23

Keywords

Center, Child, Clarity, Father, Guidance, Identity, Loss, Love, Question

Treasure Hunt

Choose a keyword that describes an area in which you are feeling confident. Write in your journal how you see yourself moving forward and leading others in that area.

Choose another keyword that describes an area in which you want to grow. Begin by writing a prayer to the Lord, seeking wisdom, direction, and steps to help you follow Him in that area. Next, write down one to three action steps you can implement today. Finally, find three verses in Scripture that speak to this area of growth, and write them in your journal.

Action Steps

- As difficult as it is, think about what life would be like if you were to lose someone close to you, perhaps your husband or child. Ask God to reveal who you are when it's just you and Him. Write down the response you hear.

- Think of a mundane task you usually dread doing and sit down and pray about it. Share with God what you don't like about the job, and ask Him to help make it enjoyable. Right after you pray, perform that task, allowing God to work in your heart as you do. Find ways to invite God into all of your chores.

- Think about the jobs you enjoy doing. What would life be like if God were to lead you in a direction that doesn't include them? Ask God to show you how much you find your identity in the work you do or the roles you play.

Prayer

Lord, thank You for calling me Your child and lavishing Your love on me. I pray You will help me see this life as the mist it is. Show me where I've put my attention, and reveal if anything is drawing me away from You. Help me commit more time to get to know You, and help me remember to invite You into everything. I pray in the mighty name of Jesus. Amen.

Keyword Search

Just to have a little fun and reinforce those keywords,
here's a little word search for you.

IDENTITY

CENTER, CHILD, CLARITY, FATHER, GUIDANCE,
IDENTITY, LOSS, LOVE, QUESTION

```
X  N  H  E  O  U  K  Y  R  E  L  V  B  B  M  N  J  W  I  F
I  C  P  Z  I  Q  T  I  B  X  O  J  Z  F  V  L  U  F  X  C
J  E  C  A  M  V  W  N  O  O  S  B  P  N  Q  J  Z  S  D  U
M  F  W  A  P  E  N  G  Y  G  S  C  L  A  R  I  T  Y  T  O
O  V  J  G  J  L  Y  A  I  H  A  O  J  G  Q  Q  L  V  L  A
P  U  Z  A  F  X  C  B  Y  E  Q  A  T  O  U  T  L  S  M  I
I  B  D  S  K  X  U  T  E  U  G  X  Q  G  E  G  O  D  P  F
W  U  H  D  S  B  X  Z  E  D  I  R  E  E  S  G  V  K  B  C
H  Q  F  M  G  X  D  Z  H  G  N  G  U  K  T  U  E  Q  L  H
H  H  I  A  F  P  N  L  A  T  W  C  G  M  I  I  F  I  A  I
U  X  Q  Q  M  Z  S  M  K  D  G  Y  Z  I  O  D  B  K  C  L
I  Z  U  B  P  J  H  W  A  C  W  I  P  H  N  A  O  S  F  D
A  Q  P  M  K  I  T  Y  H  E  A  O  L  I  L  N  Z  T  A  L
F  V  N  G  D  G  D  Y  Z  N  O  U  T  N  D  C  U  E  T  D
N  R  X  J  F  I  D  E  N  T  I  T  Y  V  T  E  Z  O  H  I
N  V  C  X  Q  W  K  M  Q  E  H  M  N  L  E  M  U  P  E  D
Q  T  F  D  K  D  U  Z  X  R  Q  X  A  Y  T  M  E  V  R  D
N  W  G  U  J  X  T  F  N  Z  B  E  O  Y  P  Y  E  G  N  W
I  V  Y  O  T  B  Y  Z  W  I  X  U  I  U  T  S  D  X  J  Z
K  X  Q  Q  W  R  E  U  X  C  Z  C  V  P  T  V  R  G  A  B
```

CHAPTER 3

Information and Expectations

H AVE YOU EVER EXPERIENCED disappointment and then later realized you learned or benefitted from the disappointing situation? During a visit from my mother-in-law, our family hoped to spend a weekend at a our favorite game reserve in South Africa. I was disappointed to discover it fully booked on both of our weekend options. Rather than moping, I searched for another resort and found one even better. It was small, so our family essentially rented out half the lodge. It felt like we were the only ones there. While it took some effort to adjust, the initial disappointment was what some would call a "blessing in disguise."

If there were ever a perfect example of unmet expectations, it would be Jews' expectations of the Messiah. Jews expected a king, and Jesus came as a servant. They expected a warrior, but He came as a peacemaker. They expected the Messiah to strike down their oppressors. Instead, Jesus said, "'Bless those who curse you, pray for those who mistreat you'" (Luke 6:28 NIV). Even for his closest followers, disappointment around Jesus peaked when He died. Talk about unmet expectations! Jews who didn't believe He was the Messiah missed out most. They allowed their disappointment to rule them and dictate how they treated Jesus and His disciples. Their anger blinded them to the incredible gift God was offering through Jesus.

No matter which way we turn, there is always the potential to disappoint someone or be disappointed. I believe we can take steps to minimize the possibility of letting others down or being let down by communicating in humility, thinking of others, asking forgiveness, seeking to understand, responding with grace, and looking for the good. Those are all ways we can walk in wisdom. As it says in Proverbs 3:13, "Happy is the man who finds wisdom, and the man *who* gains understanding" (NKJV). So let us seek to understand where we went wrong and to learn from our mistakes before trying to get others to hear us.

Key Scripture

Now as the people were in expectation, . . . John answered, saying to all, "I indeed baptize you with water; but One mightier than I is coming, whose sandal strap I am not worthy to loose. He will baptize you with the Holy Spirit and fire."

Luke 3:15–16 NKJV

Supporting Scripture

Psalms 141:3; Proverbs 18:2; Colossians 4:6; James 1:19–20

Keywords

Anger, Communication, Disappointment, Expectations, Grace, Hope, Understanding, Wisdom

Treasure Hunt

Choose a keyword that describes an area in which you are feeling confident. Write in your journal how you see yourself moving forward and leading others in that area.

Choose another keyword that describes an area in which you want to grow. Begin by writing a prayer to the Lord, seeking wisdom, direction, and steps to help you follow Him in that area. Next, write down one to three action steps you can implement today. Finally, find three verses in Scripture that speak to this area of growth, and write them in your journal.

Action Steps

- Write about a time you were disappointed by someone. List some ways you could have avoided that disappointment through communication.

- Ask the Lord to show you healthy ways to process your disappointment or sadness over unmet expectations. Write down what you hear.

- Think about how you have responded when your expectations went unmet. Ask the Lord to help you remember ways in which you responded well and ways that could have used improvement.

- Seek to understand how others see your responses to disappointment by asking your spouse or a close friend how they see you respond. Ask the Lord to show you areas in which you can grow, and ask Him to lead you in that change.

Prayer

Father God, I humble myself before You and lay all my expectations at Your feet. Please show me where I may be missing out on the good things You have for me by focusing on my disappointment. Please help me forgive those who have let me down and show me where I need to repent and seek forgiveness for my actions that have hurt others. I pray in Jesus's name. Amen.

Keyword Search

Just to have a little fun and reinforce those keywords,
here's a little word search for you.

EXPECTATIONS

ANGER, COMMUNICATION, DISAPPOINTMENT, EXPECTATIONS,
GRACE, HOPE, UNDERSTANDING, WISDOM

```
G A K F G Y C M B S D C O S K P T H H E
Z T C E X P E C T A T I O N S R C D B W
V A X W W Y Z D O K H A J D T K A D K P
F S R C J H U X I J Z N Q A F Q T N A R
J Z M P E Q I O T K X G J K R F D Q A Q
A L R R M N J T K D B E L L Q W C O W O
J I W I S D O M L S U R R U F U O X Z R
R O B I N G D I S A P P O I N T M E N T
P E J M O U T J C C J S Q V R H M T J J
X I C L Y S E V G K N H O P E O U G R U
P L Y A A I S R S D S T U J G M N O I M
F W C K R L S C N R U N L H N T I J T L
G V I U N D E R S T A N D I N G C Z W H
R P F G Y Y Y Z Z G J O D F V A C E T
V Q P A W P O B N C R V A B Z E T E E Z
Q H D D K J L A R U A Y N K F R I T K W
E S R J G W X G A J C X Y K A A O J C V
U P L L E Z M G R Q E K G I X T N K D V
F E P D R V P Z I K E F E Z U L T W L C
H Z I H I R P C Y P C C U B G O D J G D
```

CHAPTER 4

SUPPORT RAISING

MINISTRY SUPPORT COMES IN many forms, including financial and prayer. Practical support may involve providing housing, loaning a car, or providing meals. It all revolves around relationships. Raising support is less daunting if we remember that it's less about asking for money and more about inviting others into relationships.

Those who promise to pray for your ministry are just as crucial as those who agree to partner financially. Take to heart the power of prayer. Yes, financial provision is necessary, but prayer warriors are just as, if not more, important. Money won't get you through your trials; prayer will.

For example, my husband and I raised funds to purchase a car; the one we bought with those funds died completely. We couldn't raise more funds, but many people prayed. Then, after much prayer, we met a man selling a car at a price we could afford.

When Jesus sent out the seventy, He instructed them not to bring money but to trust others for food and lodging (Luke 10:4–8). The church fasted and prayed for Saul and Barnabas before sending them out on their missionary journey (Acts 13:2–3). When Moses's arms tired from holding up a rod for God's favor in battle, Aaron and Hur brought a stone for him to sit on, then they held up his arms (Exodus 17:12). These three examples are all different forms of support.

The Philippians supported Paul because of their friendship connection. There was a season when they could not give to him, but that didn't damage their friendship. In his letter, Paul affirmed that he knew they cared about him but lacked the opportunity to provide. He expressed his gratitude for their prayers, love, and relationship.

Like the Philippians, financial supporters may pause their giving for a season. It's essential to assure them that their relationship is more important than a monthly check. Paul declared that God supplies all his needs. You and I need to remember that God also provides for our needs. Sometimes, He fills those needs through other people.

Key Scripture

And you Philippians yourselves know that in the beginning of the gospel, when I left Macedonia, no church entered into partnership with me in giving and receiving, except you only. Even in Thessalonica you sent me help for my needs once and again. Not that I seek the gift, but I seek the fruit that increases to your credit.

Philippians 4:15–17

Supporting Scripture

Exodus 17:12; Luke 10:4–8; Acts 13:2–3; 2 Corinthians 9:7; Philippians 4:10–20

Keywords

Gratitude, Invitation, Partnership, Prayer, Provision, Relationships, Support, Trust

Treasure Hunt

Choose a keyword that describes an area in which you are feeling confident. Write in your journal how you see yourself moving forward and leading others in that area.

Choose another keyword that describes an area in which you want to grow. Begin by writing a prayer to the Lord, seeking wisdom, direction, and steps to help you follow Him in that area. Next, write down one to three action steps you can implement today. Finally, find three verses in Scripture that speak to this area of growth, and write them in your journal.

Action Steps

- Pray for each person you have invited to join your ministry team. Write their names as you pray, taking special care to pray for known requests. Thank the Lord for those relationships. Ask Him to bless those people, not so you might gain something more from them, but as reward for what they have offered, be it financial support or prayer.

- Choose a few people and thank them for their support with an email, handwritten note, text message, or phone call.

- As the Holy Spirit leads, reach out to others and ask how you can pray for them. If you desire, keep a separate prayer journal for ministry partnerships. Your list will get long, and compiling it may take a few days, but this exercise will remind you just how blessed you are.

Prayer

Thank You, Lord, for those who have already agreed to partner with my husband and me through prayer or financial support. I pray You will bless each one and provide for their needs as You provide for our needs through them. Thank You for those You will lead to join us in ministry in the future. Thank You for Your faithfulness in providing for our needs. I pray in Jesus's name. Amen.

Keyword Search

Just to have a little fun and reinforce those keywords,

here's a little word search for you.

CONNECTED RELATIONSHIPS

GRATITUDE, INVITATION, PARTNERSHIP, PRAYER,

PROVISION, RELATIONSHIPS, SUPPORT, TRUST

```
Y R R T R U S T Q I Z E F R E G C C V O
L V S W X P J R S Y J U K Q H G T D Q A
I N Z F I T U B H B Z K T I J D E A I K
M M Z H S Q S U P P O R T W F F Q J N O
T G E A C R Z U P R A Y E R T T J J V D
F T N I A I G M Y W R U S Y Y A E T V X
T Y R E Y E T I K E K M L H L H F K C T
C Y B Q Q R E L A T I O N S H I P S Z
W U K X V O I A O T O Z N F B G W R P U
D W M M U V S I H K O A U O O X E I Q O
K H M H C K G T P A R T N E R S H I P S
T C C Q L N R P G T C K L T Q H K H M C
L C M W X L A J K N E A I Q E P H G W F
I F Q F X L T I N V I T A T I O N D Q S
A K S C Q F I Q T O G M B Q Q T U N U A
N Q C P B K T G U F K J M R I E C F U X
D A A A C M U E M Z I U S I W Y S R E Z
H S B V I P D W Z Z C T M I W D F K S Y
C G I O W A E P R O V I S I O N H B M V
T Z O J O K K K M A J M F U U F G X J V
```

CHAPTER 5

BEING UPROOTED

I HAVE HAD MY share of goodbyes. And let me tell you, they are hard. First, my mom passed away when I was twelve, and my dad grew distant. My older siblings were already living out of the house. Then, I said goodbye to my best friend—my little brother—when I left for the Navy at eighteen. The circumstances of that season created even more loneliness. I felt a void in my life, but I didn't know what was supposed to be there.

Finally, after giving my life to Christ, I understood what had been missing: Him. I met people who filled the family void. Through matchmaking by some of them, my husband and I began our relationship. I got to know and love my wonderful parents-in-law. When I discovered I was pregnant with our first child, their first grandchild, I finally had the beautiful, full life I'd always wanted.

I entered marriage knowing that my husband and I would move overseas. But I was now part of a family, and our move affected them, too. I was not prepared to say goodbye to my new family or to raise our son away from his grandparents. I had weighed what it would cost *me* to go into missions, but I hadn't counted what it would cost others. The change was a sacrifice for all of us.

Our future was unknown. As I tried to help others understand things I didn't fully understand myself, my heart broke with each goodbye. I clung to something Jesus said: "'Everyone who has left houses or brothers or sisters or father or mother or wife or children or lands, for My name's sake, shall receive a hundredfold, and inherit eternal life'" (Matthew 19:29 NKJV).

For missionaries, uprooting our lives to live cross-culturally has its benefits. But we do it out of obedience, not for the blessings. It is difficult to leave those we love, but it would be harder *not* to chase the One we cherish above all. The ultimate reward is a relationship with Christ and eternal life with Him.

Key Scripture

So Jesus said to them, "Assuredly I say to you, that in the regeneration, when the Son of
Man sits on the throne of His glory, you who have followed Me will also sit on twelve
thrones. . . . And everyone who has left houses or brothers or sisters or father or mother
or wife or children or lands, for My name's sake, shall receive a hundredfold, and inherit
eternal life. But many who are first will be last, and the last first."
Matthew 19:28–30 NKJV

Supporting Scripture

Genesis 12:1–4; Mark 10:17–27; John 15:5; Philippians 3:17–21; 1 John 2:15–17

Keywords

Change, Goodbye, Reward, Sacrifice, Unknown, Uproot, Void

Treasure Hunt

Choose a keyword that describes an area in which you are feeling confident. Write in
your journal how you see yourself moving forward and leading others in that area.

Choose another keyword that describes an area in which you want to grow. Begin by
writing a prayer to the Lord, seeking wisdom, direction, and steps to help you follow Him
in that area. Next, write down one to three action steps you can implement today. Finally,
find three verses in Scripture that speak to this area of growth, and write them in your
journal.

Action Steps

List the people you want to say goodbye to, dividing them into three groups:

- those you *must* say goodbye to in person

- those you would *like* to say goodbye to in person as time allows

- those you *would* say goodbye to in person if you had plenty of time

Journal your thoughts about leaving America.

- Write what you feel about abandoning the American dream of laying down roots.

- Write what it means to you to be rooted in Christ and not in the world.

Make a list of the belongings you feel you will have difficulty parting with. Write out what makes letting go of the belongings seem difficult to you. As you did in chapter 1, choose a way to symbolize releasing those items.

- Write the item on a rock and throw the rock into a body of water.

- Write the item on a piece of paper and burn the paper.

- Paint the item on a canvas and paint over it.

Prayer

Father God, thank You for the material gifts You have given my husband and me. I pray for Your wisdom and guidance as we prepare to part with some things. I pray You will be with us and remind us to trust You as our provider. Please bring people to mind who are dear to us, and prepare our hearts to say goodbye well. Remind us, Lord, what it means to be uprooted from the world and rooted in You. I pray in Jesus's name. Amen.

Keyword Search

Just to have a little fun and reinforce those keywords,
here's a little word search for you.

UPROOTING

CHANGE, GOODBYE, REWARD, SACRIFICE,
UNKNOWN, UPROOT, VOID

```
A I F O E N B O K V S Q T Z Z X F R R R
O F F T Z P T Y S S K S W W K R Z T D G
D B Y R C X G H P L B L I E G P P D M M
X Y U H G X L E L Y U N E A O B U A F P
X P P A W I T K N M X O Q P O K B Z J U
Y E R Q A I U R O E I Y Y N D G K Z Q F
G M O O V B Q W L H Q N F R B E L K Y H
Z H O I A R F E C T N R D U Y Y U Q J G
T J T S D U M E G H D Y O V E K L T K P
X C H B P N R K D S A C R I F I C E K J
L S N X X K H O T R F K N Q Y W W T X M
Y M S M R N G V L E E S X Y X D C I M K
X U W N I O A A W W O U O Z X K F V Q G
W T R A F W X C H A N G E H N U Q O F P
F W H F W N D D T R Z N H D E C J I B N
Z J T R J N N R Z D A E M K D P A D B Q
C G V F P J B I K Z J O A X H C U Z I O
H A N A Q W K Y Z J M D F B X I V C H D
M E J P X X D C G B Y O W A B S V E F U
G U Z I O G I X O N G I R R V D B G H L
```

CHAPTER 6

YOUR BEST YOU

FINISHED! AS I LOGGED the last kilometer in my "Feb400" challenge, I smiled and gave myself a pat on the back. "You did it! Four hundred kilometers of walking or running in February!" I loved running, and my body felt great after that almost 250 miles, so I began planning my physical challenge for March.

My March challenge was cut short when I experienced inexplicable pain and fatigue. Over the next few months, my condition worsened, and I didn't even have the energy to go for a walk. Then, I woke up one morning to excruciating pain all over my body. I could hardly get out of bed.

A doctor who analyzed my blood and DNA discovered some discrepancies with the genetic function of my body. Fortunately, he knew of supplements that would enhance those functions. Once I started the supplements, my body began to heal, and my pain gradually disappeared. After four months on the supplements, I started walking on the treadmill. A few weeks later, I was running again. My joy through running returned!

Being unable to exercise or pick up my children because of chronic pain brought anxiety, depression, and spiritual apathy. With the pain gone, my mental clarity returned, my depression lifted, and I looked forward to getting up in the morning to spend time with God in Scripture meditation and prayer. I am more present with my family, and we can go on outings again without worrying about my pain level or fatigue.

Because I faced physical challenges, I am now acutely aware of the importance of caring for my whole being. Not just our physical bodies but our minds and hearts need care. If we suffer in one part of our being, the other parts also suffer. They are all connected.

Staying connected with the Lord gives us spiritual food to guide us through all aspects of life, and connecting with a counselor to work through grief or depression helps to improve our mental and emotional health. Attending to our minds and hearts is as important as healthy nutrition and regular exercise.

Key Scripture

I appeal to you therefore, brothers, by the mercies of God, to present your bodies as a living sacrifice, holy and acceptable to God, which is your spiritual worship. Do not be conformed to this world, but be transformed by the renewal of your mind, that by testing you may discern what is the will of God, what is good and acceptable and perfect.

Romans 12:1–2

Supporting Scripture

Matthew 22:36–40; 1 Corinthians 6:12–13, 6:19–20, 10:31; Ephesians 5:29–30

Keywords

Anxiety, Apathy, Clarity, Counselor, Depression, Emotional Health, Exercise, Mental Health, Nutrition, Prayer, Spiritual Health

Treasure Hunt

Choose a keyword that describes an area in which you are feeling confident. Write in your journal how you see yourself moving forward and leading others in that area.

Choose another keyword that describes an area in which you want to grow. Begin by writing a prayer to the Lord, seeking wisdom, direction, and steps to help you follow Him in that area. Next, write down one to three action steps you can implement today. Finally, find three verses in Scripture that speak to this area of growth, and write them in your journal.

Action Steps

- Commit to spending at least thirty minutes with God each day, reading His Word, meditating, and being still to feel His presence.

- Commit to exercising at least three times a week for thirty minutes. If you have to, do this in ten-minute increments. A brisk ten-minute walk around the house three times daily is better than nothing.

- Set a bedtime that will allow you to get eight hours of sleep each night. Give yourself a little wiggle room if this is a new thing for you. For example, if you want to be asleep by 10:00 p.m., set your bedtime for 9:30 p.m., switching off all electronics by 9:00 p.m.

- Commit to switching one meal a day to include mostly whole foods—nothing processed.

- Change out two processed snack foods this week for whole foods, such as fruits or vegetables.

- If you regularly have dessert, consider limiting desserts to one or two nights per week, giving you something to anticipate.

Prayer

Father God, I thank You that I am fearfully and wonderfully made. Thank you for all the intricate details of my being—my emotions, body, and spirit. Please show me areas where I may not be practicing good self-care. Show me where I may begin to form new habits to improve how I care for and love myself. Help me prioritize my relationship with you, build my spiritual health, and love others well. I pray in Jesus's name. Amen.

Keyword Search

Just to have a little fun and reinforce those keywords,
here's a little word search for you.

SELF-CARE

ANXIETY, APATHY, CLARITY, COUNSELOR, DEPRESSION,
EMOTIONAL HEALTH, EXERCISE, MENTAL HEALTH,
NUTRITION, PRAYER, SPIRITUAL HEALTH

```
A H O M H D A W J W J C O U N S E L O R
N V H A E M O T I O N A L H E A L T H F
X V O O Q B K E N U T R I T I O N J A M
I I C L A R I T Y M Z X L N M J R F B Q
E G G M P G B V Z J Q L M D U K Q G A S
T Q U L A C O Y D P W T W E R Z C Z N P
Y E D W T V R D U Q Q E U P R Q J B A I
E E N Z H I U D G K J X Q R Q G I F N R
F W T Y Y S Q Q U H W E E E J J O I K I
G W R D E Q O Y V R F R Q S K T M X M T
Y X N I M T Y O H V C C W S T Y D J L U
K S A A Y G J Q C P G I O I H Y D Z V A
H B T R R L N N C T T S Z O C K S B O L
P C L V T P M K P J C E E N Z B C K Q H
H N C P S P R A Y E R W J J Z C Y K X E
I P L A H K A Q K B R V L E Q Y K C U A
A L G V I G M F G G E H O O A J H E U L
Z P G G L D I E A T N G K T K V F X E T
O O W F K E K J M E N T A L H E A L T H
X M T L G G D S H R Q X G J I F D E A F
```

CHAPTER 7

TIME TO FLY

W HEN WE MOVED TO Africa, I wanted to get the travel out of the way and just get where we were going. That mentality led to physical and mental exhaustion. I hardly remember our journey at all. In hindsight, and after many more international trips, I have learned that travel can and should be as fun as arriving at our destination.

When I am getting ready to travel for a move or a short trip, the first thing I do is pray. I then write out our itinerary for the entire trip, including departure, arrival, and boarding times and things to do at the airports: places to eat, where the kids can play, and places to rest. I pray over that itinerary. As it says in Joshua 1:9, "'The Lord your God is with you wherever you go.'" When we invite Him into our planning, He guides our steps.

Next, I estimate how much time we'll have for each leg of the journey and list things we need to do and fun stuff we could do if time allows. I outline things we will need to do shortly after arrival to limit how many decisions are made under the effects of jet lag. While my schedules and lists are helpful, we are not bound to them. I do all this knowing that our plans may change due to things beyond our control. At least we have a point of reference and can make an informed decision if we need to change something.

Spiritual attacks come when we are tired or distracted. A detailed travel plan that includes rest, exploration, and play guides us when we are too tired to think or make decisions. Jesus knew the toll traveling had on His apostles, physically and spiritually. He said, "'Come away by yourselves to a desolate place and rest a while'" (Mark 6:31). Though we've come a long way in modes of travel since Jesus's day, getting rest is still an essential component of any journey. Traveling shouldn't bring anxiety. It should be enjoyable and filled with God's peace.

Key Scripture

The apostles returned to Jesus and told him all that they had done and taught. And he said to them, "Come away by yourselves to a desolate place and rest a while." For many were coming and going, and they had no leisure even to eat. And they went away in the boat to a desolate place by themselves.

Mark 6:30–32

Supporting Scripture

Joshua 1:9; Philippians 4:5b–7

Keywords

Anxiety, Distractions, Exhaustion, Peace, Planning, Prayer, Prioritize, Rest, Spiritual Attack

Treasure Hunt

Choose a keyword that describes an area in which you are feeling confident. Write in your journal how you see yourself moving forward and leading others in that area.

Choose another keyword that describes an area in which you want to grow. Begin by writing a prayer to the Lord, seeking wisdom, direction, and steps to help you follow Him in that area. Next, write down one to three action steps you can implement today. Finally, find three verses in Scripture that speak to this area of growth, and write them in your journal.

Action Steps

Make a list of things you would like to do while you travel. Dream big! You can narrow it down to realistic possibilities later. Will you plan to explore along the way? Schedule in a hotel for rest and a shower?

If you have your travel itinerary, take time to make a general outline, including

- airports you will go through and what is available in each

- when and where you will rest during your travel

- which activities from your list are possible, and when

Make a list of the things about travel that make you feel anxious. Commit each one to prayer and ask God to give you peace and show you how to reframe your thinking about each item.

Prayer

Father God, I thank You that you pave the way for my husband and me, and we can trust You to go before us, with us, and behind us as we prepare to travel. I pray that You will be with us in our planning and assist us in making our travel as enjoyable as possible. I pray You will take our anxiety and help us to adapt as we go. Show us Your glory through what we experience in every aspect of our journey. I pray in Jesus's name. Amen.

Keyword Search

Just to have a little fun and reinforce those keywords,
here's a little word search for you.

TRAVEL

ANXIETY, DISTRACTIONS, EXHAUSTION, PEACE, PLANNING,
PRAYER, PRIORITIZE, REST, SPIRITUAL ATTACK

```
G M E X H A U S T I O N O A S P O B I V
A V H U I M A X G P B J J Y R P L Y T M
I A O E L R K K H L B V C F D A I W C Q
L B L Z R Z P L S D A L Z S W J T J Q Q
S L Y L H K L C D I K A F L D D N U B P
W T P O T T U L C S Q I M W G F S V L M
C S P R A Y E R D T D F P J P I I H J O
G S L D O P B D B R D V R Y R M X P C T
L M L C U P D R C A Q T I Y U Q O V A Z
W H B N J A X A E C J I O E T L A H N D
H W Z P Y O Q O R T U X R U D O T C X Y
Z A X O L Y P Y A I G T I L E F L D I V
L Z D T X C L U K O V F T T Y B Q J E Y
Z W T V L C A F H N D L I A V S M P T V
K S Y O I L N L C S D H Z B P O W E Y G
V A W X A U N E C K E K E X U Z R A J S
S J P V S P I R I T U A L A T T A C K O
G H T Y X U N H K V L O T O J J K E V R
S Z Y K C H G P X V S O B M B U R U M Q
H M C L R E S T V E T F H W R K X X R E
```

CHAPTER 8

SETTLING IN

THEME: FINDING HOME

A T A WRITERS' CONFERENCE I attended virtually, a speaker talked about the Garden of Eden as our original home, to which we each want to return with the whole of our being. Stuck in the alternate reality we were born into, we have learned to obey the rules of this reality and to do what others expect of us. Moving to a foreign culture is much like that. We were born into one culture, and then we choose to explore or live in another. In a culture different from what we are used to, we need to learn new behaviors and rules.

Since being married and starting a family, I have lived in a house with my family and called it home, but that house is not our home. Having moved so many times, the word *home* holds different meanings for me. Essentially, my home is wherever my family and I are together. For instance, when we travel on vacation and rent a house from someone else, we call that house "home" because that's where we are together for that time.

Some have expected us to purchase a house to provide our children a sense of home, a firm grasp on who they are, and where they belong. But I fear that could keep our children grounded in the world. We want to teach them not to be of this world but to seek God's world and to trust Him.

Setting up a comfortable living space here on earth provides a shelter from the elements and a sanctuary when life's stressors come crashing down. However, it's important to remember that our physical houses cannot compare with the heavenly home the Lord has prepared for us. I believe it is that heavenly home all of us long for when we crave that sense of familiarity, security, and shelter—things only God can provide. Home is where God is. Understanding home in that way gives a whole new meaning to the saying "Home is where the heart is." If our hearts are with God, then there our home will be.

Key Scripture

Whoever dwells in the shelter of the Most High will rest in the shadow of the Almighty.
I will say of the LORD, "He is my refuge and my fortress, my God, in whom I trust."
Psalms 91:1–2

Supporting Scripture

John 14:2, 15:18–19; Colossians 2:6–7, 3:2

Keywords

Comfort, Familiarity, Home, Roots, Sanctuary, Security, Shelter, Trust

Treasure Hunt

Choose a keyword that describes an area in which you are feeling confident. Write in your journal how you see yourself moving forward and leading others in that area.

Choose another keyword that describes an area in which you want to grow. Begin by writing a prayer to the Lord, seeking wisdom, direction, and steps to help you follow Him in that area. Next, write down one to three action steps you can implement today. Finally, find three verses in Scripture that speak to this area of growth, and write them in your journal.

Action Steps

- Look around your home. Write down a list of three or four things that you can physically see that give you a sense or feeling of home. Then list three or four things that you can't see with your eyes but that give you a sense or feeling of home.

- Reflecting on this chapter's key Scripture, draw a picture or design word art that represents you dwelling in the shelter of the Most High.

Prayer

Father God, I am thankful I can make You my fortress, shelter, and stronghold. I pray that no matter where in the world my family and I make our dwelling, our hearts will never forget that our home is in You. I pray You will go before us and prepare houses that serve as sanctuaries and respites where we can release our stress and refresh our spirits. I pray that You will fill those buildings with Your Spirit and Your peace and place a hedge of protection around them so that nothing that is not of You may enter them.

Keyword Search

Just to have a little fun and reinforce those keywords,
here's a little word search for you.

FINDING HOME

COMFORT, FAMILIARITY, HOME, ROOTS,
SANCTUARY, SECURITY, SHELTER, TRUST

```
F  R  Q  L  D  C  Z  M  E  E  H  Z  T  X  P  G  Y  Y  C  U
K  U  Y  A  Y  D  E  Z  S  L  D  O  T  R  U  S  T  Y  M  O
R  G  K  P  X  S  B  L  A  C  Q  Q  V  A  U  Q  R  E  E  E
F  Q  M  J  O  Y  I  D  X  H  N  M  I  O  D  V  H  F  C  Y
P  A  Y  R  V  C  A  K  Z  E  E  L  H  T  B  N  R  A  R  O
I  Y  C  D  J  J  I  S  H  E  L  T  E  R  S  J  M  M  I  K
K  R  N  P  L  F  W  U  X  U  I  J  T  K  A  C  K  I  H  G
S  P  A  J  P  V  J  R  F  G  Q  V  J  E  V  P  T  L  F  R
X  W  E  K  E  Y  A  V  Z  N  T  P  I  B  G  G  L  I  V  O
D  D  N  O  K  Y  E  Q  J  L  J  Q  K  J  A  F  K  A  M  O
Q  C  Z  Z  W  W  H  S  E  C  U  R  I  T  Y  L  L  R  D  T
W  E  P  K  W  F  O  M  G  Y  A  Q  X  F  D  W  L  I  A  S
R  K  N  S  L  X  Z  X  F  V  T  Q  R  L  Z  B  S  T  N  Y
Y  Z  S  L  S  L  F  Z  N  F  F  U  B  I  Y  D  Z  Y  B  Y
N  R  Q  U  C  G  I  H  R  F  E  Y  D  U  R  Q  M  F  K  P
C  O  M  F  O  R  T  Z  G  P  O  P  N  G  H  A  A  F  Q  H
P  T  P  J  O  L  X  B  Z  O  S  S  J  U  X  P  S  Y  A  F
W  Q  J  J  G  H  C  H  O  H  E  O  D  D  K  A  W  Q  M  W
M  Y  I  O  W  T  Y  A  T  E  S  A  N  C  T  U  A  R  Y  F
E  H  O  M  E  N  D  O  O  D  G  V  B  P  F  I  F  E  K  R
```

CHAPTER 9

LIVING LIFE WITH OTHERS

THEME: BEING COMMUNITY

T HE CALL DISCONNECTED BEFORE I could answer. "Did you butt-dial me?" I jokingly texted. My friend's quick reply caught me off guard. "No. Emergency!" When my phone rang again, I didn't hesitate to answer. "What's up? Are you okay?" I was preparing to take someone to the hospital.

Then my friend explained what happened. She had left the house that morning confident in her preparations. She remembered all their passports, loaded all four kids in the car, and headed across the border to pick up a few things. A feat to be proud of, indeed. But when she went to pay for something, she realized she'd forgotten her purse at home. She had no ID besides her passport, no cash or cards. She was stuck in South Africa since she couldn't pay the border toll to get back into Lesotho.

I recalled the many times I needed help when we first moved to Lesotho. Now, it was my turn to help. "Can your husband meet you?" I asked calmly—easier now, knowing we weren't going to the hospital. "No, I have his passport," she replied quickly.

"Okay, don't panic." After more brainstorming, I suggested I could meet her at the border post with cash for the border toll. "At least you can get home." We had a plan. I told my kids to get dressed, and we headed to the border. My friend made it to the border post just fine. I gave her money for the toll, and she was on her way.

Being a community is showing love in many ways, from border rescues, preparing meals, picking something up since we're already out, running someone to the hospital, and holding one another accountable. My friend was not in physical danger, but she was emotionally overwhelmed. The opportunity to respond to her call also blessed me. Knowing I could be of service in someone's time of need assured me I had community, too. I could give back for all the times we've been in need.

Key Scripture

Two are better than one, because they have a good reward for their toil. For if they fall, one will lift up his fellow. But woe to him who is alone when he falls and has not another to lift him up! Again, if two lie together, they keep warm, but how can one keep warm alone? And though a man might prevail against one who is alone, two will withstand him—a threefold cord is not quickly broken.

Ecclesiastes 4:9–12

Supporting Scripture

John 13:34–35; Romans 1:11–12; 1 Thessalonians 5:11; 1 Peter 4:8–11

Keywords

Accountability, Community, Help, Love, Need, Support, Opportunity, Overwhelm

Treasure Hunt

Choose a keyword that describes an area in which you are feeling confident. Write in your journal how you see yourself moving forward and leading others in that area.

Choose another keyword that describes an area in which you want to grow. Begin by writing a prayer to the Lord, seeking wisdom, direction, and steps to help you follow Him in that area. Next, write down one to three action steps you can implement today. Finally, find three verses in Scripture that speak to this area of growth, and write them in your journal.

Action Steps

Write down three ways you know you could be of service to others, then pray for opportunities to use those gifts in your community.

Think of a time when you needed help in the past. Write down the details of the situation and answer these questions:

- Was it difficult to ask for or accept someone's help?

- How did it make you feel when someone responded and provided for you?

- Did you immediately look for a way to repay the helper?

If you struggle to ask for help, pray for the courage to start stretching yourself now. Think of one or two ways you could ask someone for help this week. After receiving help, journal how the experience made you feel.

Prayer

Father God, thank You for providing a helpful community to love and support me. Please show me areas of gifting through which I may contribute to my community. As I plan to go overseas, I pray You will prepare my heart and the hearts of those who will be serving alongside me so we may be of service to each other. Please give me the courage to ask for help when I need it, so I may give others opportunities to serve.

Keyword Search

Just to have a little fun and reinforce those keywords,
here's a little word search for you.

BEING COMMUNITY

ACCOUNTABILITY, COMMUNITY, HELP, LOVE,
NEED, OPPORTUNITY, OVERWHELM, SUPPORT

```
T  T  W  W  L  C  K  H  O  S  D  E  D  B  I  A  F  X  K  L
T  N  S  X  O  P  P  O  R  T  U  N  I  T  Y  Q  C  Y  D  H
N  O  G  B  N  U  B  E  G  S  B  P  T  Z  P  H  D  X  S  G
J  H  K  F  L  H  A  C  C  O  U  N  T  A  B  I  L  I  T  Y
Q  Q  P  E  E  X  V  A  T  X  N  C  S  U  P  P  O  R  T  J
X  V  B  W  C  W  L  Y  M  J  I  Z  H  K  S  S  Q  Z  Z  Z
V  Q  M  H  S  B  Q  A  F  B  F  K  T  L  C  J  A  O  G  H
F  R  C  O  M  M  U  N  I  T  Y  O  T  D  Y  Y  Q  U  Y  P
W  N  H  L  Z  J  N  L  A  F  Z  M  W  G  Q  D  M  Q  Z  L
E  H  C  Y  O  P  M  B  X  O  O  C  Y  M  H  O  H  D  N  I
T  I  G  J  V  V  F  X  P  B  U  E  N  F  W  T  O  S  V  Y
S  T  V  L  E  D  L  Q  K  O  P  D  V  O  E  W  E  N  F  T
Q  Z  A  L  R  G  I  H  U  R  T  G  I  I  V  L  Q  O  T  U
L  O  D  W  W  V  P  Y  X  P  H  U  B  S  L  X  Z  N  T  X
O  B  J  O  H  R  Y  V  U  L  T  V  Z  S  Y  J  L  E  K  Z
V  X  D  S  E  G  T  S  J  R  E  N  E  E  D  U  I  E  N  W
E  E  D  G  L  N  B  E  B  X  Z  N  D  R  W  X  D  X  A  V
A  I  F  R  M  M  L  J  F  D  W  C  U  W  G  H  E  L  P  Y
K  V  Q  I  K  V  P  T  T  X  K  D  H  Y  S  H  N  V  L  X
U  V  L  W  A  O  Z  D  P  Y  M  Z  H  J  M  Y  U  V  K  M
```

CHAPTER 10

SPIRITUAL WARFARE

THEME: ANCHORED

I NEVER EXPECTED A phone call could send me to a place of spiritual warfare. A friend called me to let me know I'd hurt her feelings with something I had failed to do. It was something I had thought about doing and should have done, but I still didn't do it. I messed up, and I felt horrible. When we got off the phone, I started analyzing other areas of my life where I felt like I was failing—as a mother, wife, friend, teammate, or writer. Tallying all the mistakes I've made since giving my life to Christ, I berated myself.

- *Why am I still struggling with the same things after all these years?*

- *Why am I still so far from being who God created me to be?*

- *Why do I still have negative thoughts about who I am in Christ?*

This thought pattern sent me into a dark place and gave the enemy a foothold to attack my very existence. He exploited my weaknesses, suggesting I was wasting space, that I should not be here anymore, and that everyone would be better off if I weren't. I believed all the negative things the enemy said about me because he used my recurring struggles against me. He's not clever, just manipulative.

Then he tried to make me believe that God wasn't good, wouldn't be there for me, and wouldn't help me. When my husband arrived home, I shared my struggle, and he prayed over me, spoke truth over me, and encouraged me through God's Word. The blessing of having others who will pray for me, coupled with the foundation of faith I have built with God over the years, kept me grounded in His truth in an hour of desperation when the enemy had a firm hold on me.

Having our hearts rooted in Christ by establishing a solid relationship with God is like an anchor tethering us to the truth when the enemy tries to pull us into the undercurrent of darkness. God is our hope when things seem lost, our light when things seem dark.

Key Scripture

"Everyone then who hears these words of mine and does them will be like a wise man who built his house on the rock. And the rain fell, and the floods came, and the winds blew and beat on that house, but it did not fall, because it had been founded on the rock."

Matthew 7:24–25

Supporting Scripture

Luke 10:19–20; John 16:33; Ephesians 6:10–18; 1 John 5:4–5

Keywords

Anchor, Darkness, Faith, Foundation, Hope, Light, Manipulation, Spiritual Battle, Truth

Treasure Hunt

Choose a keyword that describes an area in which you are feeling confident. Write in your journal how you see yourself moving forward and leading others in that area.

Choose another keyword that describes an area in which you want to grow. Begin by writing a prayer to the Lord, seeking wisdom, direction, and steps to help you follow Him in that area. Next, write down one to three action steps you can implement today. Finally, find three verses in Scripture that speak to this area of growth, and write them in your journal.

Action Steps

- Commit to spending at least fifteen minutes in God's Word each day. Continue to anchor yourself in the truth of God's Word and establish a firm foundation of faith.

- Set at least one reminder for the middle of your day to remind you to bring Scripture to mind.

- Make a list of people who will be there to pray with you, pray for you, and pray over you to pull you through dark moments when they come.

- Write out a prayer you can pray over yourself to remind you that you are a child of God, are filled with the Holy Spirit, and have a purpose in this world.

Prayer

Father God, thank You that I am part of Your holy family. I pray You would give me wisdom and guidance as I seek to hide Your Word in my heart. I pray that You help me find a counselor, trusted friends, and prayer warriors to help build me up when the enemy attacks. Please draw me to You as I continue to anchor myself in the truth of Your Word and to establish a firm foundation of faith. Prepare me for the spiritual warfare I will face. I pray in Jesus's name. Amen.

Keyword Search

Just to have a little fun and reinforce those keywords,
here's a little word search for you.

ANCHORED

ANCHOR, DARKNESS, FAITH, FOUNDATION, HOPE,
LIGHT, MANIPULATION, SPIRITUAL BATTLE, TRUTH

```
G  Y  Z  J  D  S  W  C  L  Y  A  N  C  H  O  R  R  V  P  J
J  L  P  D  A  G  E  U  S  S  C  F  A  I  T  H  S  B  O  M
F  J  Q  F  G  I  P  U  Z  F  X  T  S  D  J  P  L  N  E  O
I  N  Q  O  W  D  R  H  T  V  D  Q  J  R  H  R  C  O  Z  A
W  C  Y  U  M  O  J  B  O  V  A  N  S  V  R  T  Z  S  I  H
R  L  D  N  H  W  S  A  T  Z  S  V  H  H  J  T  U  E  I  G
M  V  Y  D  A  N  R  X  R  Y  J  D  M  I  M  V  V  E  R  L
Q  E  H  A  B  L  V  P  U  W  I  B  J  Z  K  J  Z  P  F  V
H  D  N  T  L  I  G  H  T  R  E  T  C  T  X  Q  Z  B  I  C
M  A  P  I  X  C  O  M  H  A  I  T  Y  S  W  H  V  C  Z  I
X  R  T  O  F  V  P  Y  T  B  Q  Y  I  X  E  R  I  I  P  J
W  K  K  N  R  I  Z  Q  E  P  F  D  Z  U  Z  Y  B  P  M  P
E  N  H  H  S  B  L  M  M  A  N  I  P  U  L  A  T  I  O  N
G  E  Z  M  N  P  J  P  N  A  R  W  T  V  V  S  J  T  V  I
M  S  L  H  P  S  Z  H  H  V  U  P  K  A  M  S  R  A  Q  K
F  S  P  I  R  I  T  U  A  L  B  A  T  T  L  E  R  G  Z  C
N  A  P  Z  P  J  B  K  Y  V  O  Z  I  E  F  C  J  M  P  N
V  C  V  W  I  M  P  S  D  V  A  M  W  I  U  H  U  A  G  F
R  N  R  W  D  W  Y  J  K  M  Y  A  D  M  L  W  F  G  M  I
O  K  E  B  V  R  D  D  H  O  P  E  M  Y  L  Y  I  U  Z  C
```

CHAPTER 11

LIFE AFTER DEATH

THEME: REJOICE NOW

ALL OF US HAVE or will experience grief. We grieve losing a loved one, losing hope of seeing a dream fulfilled, or losing the ability to do something. Having walked through many forms of grief, I have learned to look for "redemption markers"—little reminders that God is in control, so I can "Rejoice in hope, be patient in tribulation, be constant in prayer" (Romans 12:12). It's a way of trusting He will bring good from what is lost.

When we began our adoption application, I was still grieving the loss of three pregnancies and the hope of ever having another baby through pregnancy. Once the adoption of our daughter, Isabella, was complete, we entered a new season of grief—delayed gratification. The United States requires having custody for two years before applying for an immigration visa. During that time, God spoke to us about changing our ministry to be in the United States. As we waited, we dreamed of her life and opportunities once we returned to America. Once we completed our application, we thought the process would be relatively quick and easy. We were mistaken.

As of this writing, we have been waiting over two additional years to hear news about our immigration petition. Through this process, we are leaning on God more and finding our hope and completeness in Him. We are growing in our relationship with Him and living more in the present and less in the future. If we continued to focus on the difficulty of the season and only looked forward to the end, we would miss all we could learn in the midst of it.

Sometimes hope feels distant when walking through pain, darkness, or the unknown. We might question God's goodness or our purpose and miss the blessings and gifts still around us. Through each season of grief, sorrow, and waiting, we've been able to look around to see the gifts around us and the ways God carried us through the dark, lighting our path. Walking through grief can seem like the end of the world for many people. But if you're still alive, it's not the end, and God still has good things for you.

Key Scripture

Rejoice in hope, be patient in tribulation, be constant in prayer.

Romans 12:12

Supporting Scripture

Isaiah 61:1–3; John 11:3–4, 11:40–42, 14:26; Romans 8:28; 1 Thessalonians 5:18; James
1:2–4, 1:12; 1 Peter 4:12–13

Keywords

Dreams, Grief, Growing, Hope, Patience, Purpose, Redemption, Rejoice, Sorrow, Trust

Treasure Hunt

Choose a keyword that describes an area in which you are feeling confident. Write in
your journal how you see yourself moving forward and leading others in that area.

Choose another keyword that describes an area in which you want to grow. Begin by
writing a prayer to the Lord, seeking wisdom, direction, and steps to help you follow Him
in that area. Next, write down one to three action steps you can implement today. Finally,
find three verses in Scripture that speak to this area of growth, and write them in your
journal.

Action Steps

- Journal about a time when you faced a particularly difficult trial.

- Write out what you learned from going through that trial. Try to remember and write down small glimpses of redemption markers you saw while in the midst of your grief or difficulty.

- Thank the Lord for your experience, the ways you saw His hand working through it, and what you learned from it.

Prayer

Father God, thank You that you never waste a hurt. Thank you that even in the middle of my sorrow, You are working things for my good. I am grateful I can rest in the knowledge that I will come away from my trials stronger and more reliant on You. Lord, You are so good, and I praise Your name. I pray I will count it pure joy when I face trials and will remember to notice even the small moments of redemption. I pray in Jesus's name. Amen.

Keyword Search

Just to have a little fun and reinforce those keywords,

here's a little word search for you.

REJOICE NOW

DREAMS, GRIEF, GROWING, HOPE, PATIENCE, PURPOSE,
REDEMPTION, REJOICE, SORROW, TRUST

```
U  B  P  E  L  R  L  H  G  J  T  H  E  U  G  N  G  Y  M  H
P  F  D  F  A  J  M  O  J  S  H  M  O  V  R  R  T  A  O  F
W  E  K  F  A  N  I  P  J  C  W  P  A  T  I  E  N  C  E  B
H  H  F  H  P  I  L  E  A  Z  B  X  S  S  E  J  R  I  P  L
Q  Y  K  C  W  W  F  Z  X  L  J  M  D  E  F  O  E  E  I  X
L  E  Z  U  G  J  K  G  X  L  W  O  Z  M  M  I  J  W  R  M
R  P  Q  R  G  N  N  P  P  L  C  K  P  Z  S  C  E  S  A  V
F  Z  L  O  A  G  R  O  W  I  N  G  C  T  N  E  N  G  P  Z
J  H  L  Y  X  S  E  P  Q  Q  P  K  S  O  R  R  O  W  N  T
Y  Q  X  K  K  Q  D  Y  A  A  Q  P  V  M  W  X  K  H  Q  I
N  H  H  Y  V  P  E  W  F  W  T  C  H  W  B  P  S  X  P  W
U  X  F  Q  A  G  M  A  P  H  M  E  S  J  L  Q  O  N  D  W
R  S  R  A  Z  Y  P  S  T  P  Y  S  M  Z  X  C  Z  P  R  X
H  U  U  R  I  G  T  R  I  A  P  U  H  R  F  L  T  U  E  X
W  M  V  K  N  K  I  C  O  B  P  S  R  F  F  Y  R  R  A  U
B  U  I  B  I  N  O  Y  W  K  C  B  W  E  C  X  U  P  M  H
X  J  I  T  F  S  N  Z  Q  G  Y  M  V  D  A  V  S  O  S  O
W  Q  A  V  K  R  P  T  G  U  X  W  U  O  O  O  T  S  Z  Z
P  W  X  O  X  B  G  R  C  B  U  L  L  R  C  O  J  E  T  S
D  Y  G  J  O  P  A  B  I  Y  G  A  P  R  A  P  J  S  J  V
```

Closing Prayer

FATHER GOD, THANK YOU for my friend who has gone through this workbook with me. I pray You will watch over her as she prepares to go on the mission field to spread the good news of the Gospel and to serve others in Your holy name. Help her to submit and release her plans and ideas to You and trust You to reveal Your plans. Remind her each day of who You are and who she is as a child of the King. I pray you will bring ministry partners who will financially and prayerfully support her in ministry. Help her to see expectations that may be unknown, that she would recognize her response if they go unmet. Prepare her heart for the difficulty of saying goodbye and the adventure of life in a new culture with a new community. Help her remember to prioritize her whole health and realize that it's difficult to serve others well if she is not well. As she prepares to travel, I pray you will guide her in planning and go ahead of her to make the journey enjoyable and memorable. Give her wisdom, clarity, and creativity to prepare her new sanctuary. When tensions arise in her marriage, encourage her to pray for her husband and remember he is not her enemy. Guide her heart as she feasts on your Word. Help her keep the truth in her heart to easily recall it when the enemy tries to feed her lies. I pray You will prepare her heart for what is ahead and show her glimpses of Your glory through whatever season or trial she walks through. Prepare her heart and mind for battle, Lord. I pray in the mighty name of Jesus. Amen.

THANK YOU

T HANK YOU FOR TAKING this journey of going deeper into God's Word and preparing yourself for missionary service in a foreign culture. I pray that the Lord revealed your strengths and areas for growth and that you enacted steps to bring you closer to the likeness of Jesus, our mutual aim. May the Lord continually bless you on your journey.

If you have enjoyed *Living Uprooted* and this companion workbook, please write reviews for both on Amazon to help boost the discoverability of these resources.

I offer more encouragement through my website, www.marieygabroad.com, where you can sign up to receive my monthly newsletter. You may also follow me on social media at www.facebook.com/marikeygabroad.

ABOUT THE AUTHOR

A FORMER MASSAGE THERAPIST, personal trainer, and physical therapist assistant, Mari Eygabroad planned to use her skills in Africa alongside her pilot/mechanic husband. God had a different calling. During the first few of ten years serving overseas with Mission Aviation Fellowship, Mari felt unequipped for the many hardships her family faced. She wrote *Living Uprooted* and the companion workbook as training materials for women going into overseas missions alongside their husbands. Mari and her family live in Lesotho, Southern Africa.

ABOUT THE AUTHOR

Just to have a little fun getting to know the author, here's one last word search for you with a few of her favorite things.

```
Y A R D L J P U U B R T E F T E D X B O
P W C H R I S T M A S G S V N N B J U A      BRYAN
L I S A B E L L A G K M S R N J R E S P
I K T H N E X E K I M G H K U M Y S T R      CHOCOLATE
C D D C Z S X G N E W M L M H N A U G K
R Q O O N K M Q W W N A W O U P N S B C      CHRISTMAS
N Y H S I C N W E J F T F U J S I I K L
Q N C G F C Y L N H D T J N E T H X N Y      COFFEE
D I H J A T H P M Z A H P T Q J F A H G
F A S B Z I Q O A L W I E A V T Q U L Q      HIKING
O U K K U K P E C P Y A B I G U F W T M
J A V V K J N E X O S S D N W N N A A P      ISABELLA
B O I T R G R P F T L U Y S V A L Z J D
P W J E W P J P C M N A G J J B H O B Q      JESUS
K D A H M D Y H L A S D T W N K Y R B J
Q X T I E T G D N C O F F E E C R C S P      MATTHIAS
I V Z K Z V P A D Y B G C H L N W L C K
P M E I R T Q S N F Q M H F D Y N K S M      MOUNTAINS
U R H N M K L C J F P J Z M U I J P P J
L N I G F K H B P S I O M O P Z C R P T      RUNNING
```

ACKNOWLEDGMENTS

This workbook has been a project of love and wouldn't be possible without help.

Thank you to my husband, Bryan, for allowing me to take time away from the family to write.

Thank you to my kids, Matthias and Isabella, for behaving for your daddy while I worked.

Thanks to my writing group—the Lady Lits—Janet, Jill, Linda, Nancy, Sarah, and Susan. Your inspiration, encouragement, and insight helped this project come together. I'm so grateful for all I've learned from each of you.

Thanks to my content editor, Melanie Chitwood, Harvest House author of *What a Husband Needs from His Wife*, writer, writing coach, and editor at www.melanieschit wood.com, and my copyeditor, JB Wilson.

And thank you, my readers and followers, for sharing these books and blog posts to keep the encouragement going.

Cross and Lion Books